This journal belongs to

Introduction

Earth warriors are part of a new spiritual generation. They are a unique soul group, united by shared qualities, rather than by age, culture, gender, religion or philosophy. Earth warriors are particularly respectful and honouring of the sacred feminine in her form as Mother Earth. They are kind and loving, especially towards animals and human beings that need additional protection from abuses of power. Earth warriors are a beautiful combination of gentleness, wisdom and fierce, sacred rage that gives them a courageous voice and enough awareness to stand up and make the truth known. This may be through activism, education or sharing information about political agendas, the truth behind advertising or unethical business practices. Earth warriors are truth speakers, and it is loving kindness that motivates them to be sacred rebels.

Earth warriors are the guardians and way-showers of the new world — of a new human culture based on the sacred wisdom of protection, connection, respect, love and spiritual integrity. They see right through the false glitter of status or object worship. They are interested in what is real for the soul. They prioritise relationships and the support of the tribe above money and worldly power, and because of this, they have spiritual empowerment. They emit a certain type of heart light that helps humanity to remember what truly matters. They hold the power of certainty that when we use our voice, our talents, our hearts and whatever we have at our disposal for the greater good, things happen, situations change, and we need not feel intimidated nor silenced by forces of greed, hate or fear.

The earth warrior is not just about keeping his or her patch of earth clean and sacred. They want to inspire, teach, protect and encourage as many humans as possible to join the fray and say no to what goes against the wisdom of the heart. Earth warriors are the soul conscience of humanity.

Some years ago, I was drawn to sing mantras in larger groups of people and was invited to sing at a drumming circle. I wasn't a drummer, but I love to dance, have good rhythm, and they were open to all sorts of musical offerings. So, I took my crystal singing bowls and my voice to what was the first session of many years of mantra healings, new friendships and dancing to freestyle djembe drumming. It was a breath of fresh air for my soul, and I felt a kinship with the wild and free spirits that were part of that community. Over the years, I worked with a number of those beautiful people in musical performances and got to know them and their unique social culture. These people who were living (quite literally drumming!) to their own rhythms created such an impression on me.

As a rebel who marches to my own beat, I could totally relate to them. Although I had a strong sense of spiritual community, in many ways I was also quite a loner and hermit for large portions of my life. This suited me. It gave me time to contemplate, reflect and give birth to new ideas. I enjoy my time socialising and being in connection with others, but I also take delight in solitude. It is a regular part of my lifestyle and I find it very restorative. This community intrigued me, because they were so different to me in this way. They were very communal and community focused. There was a sense that their entire tribe — and I would call it a tribe for this reason — was one spiritual body, with many individual members. In the same way we have a body that is made up of arms, legs, heart, brain and so on, this tribal soul body had its parts, and yet, it was one being.

Their values of leaving no trace, of loving the earth, of protecting the environment and of supporting each other in their individual journeys of personal development — whether it be self-healing, yoga practice, teaching, tantra or music, for example — without any judgement whatsoever, was astonishing to me. I had lived in communities rife with political backstabbing and power games, and yet here I had stumbled into a tribal family spread all over Sydney, with some hundred members or so, with so much genuine encouragement for each other, so absent of ego … I felt a bit like a spiritual anthropologist discovering a rare tribe, and I was fascinated!

There were problems to be dealt with, of course. Pain and struggle are part of life, even lives well lived with awareness. Still, it was one of the healthiest human ecosystems that I had ever encountered, and I have been in and out of many groups over the years, with many claiming to be spiritually evolved. I loved that this group didn't claim anything more than being a type of family based in love and respect, and this seemed very true to my experience of that community.

In time I learned to recognise this tribal frequency. As I travelled, I found those same frequencies in other parts of the world. This tribal consciousness was a global movement rather than something unique to that one beautiful community I was led to in Australia. Some groups looked like they should belong to that tribal consciousness, and yet lacked the real heart. On the surface, other groups seemed to have little in common, but held the same genuine heart frequency. There were people of all ages and walks of life that were drawn to these types of communities and the ways of being that they naturally create, as they recognised the value of what they bring to the earth.

This generation instinctively recognises that if we allow the powers-that-be to determine our values and where we place our time and energy, all that is precious in life will be destroyed. This realisation is not 'overly dramatic' but acknowledged as fact, and the response is not despair, but creativity. This generation opts out of so much consumerism and so much anxiety-inducing status-worship. They choose to be real, to honour their own souls and live from the heart. They feel no need to live up to the expectations imposed on them by a sick social system. They create their own spiritual standards and encourage each other without shaming or guilt. They are accepting, but set boundaries based on what matters to them. These earth warriors are the saviours, guides, defenders and wise wayshowers who carry eagle vision and the medicine of the wolf teacher that ensures future generations will have access to something worth protecting.

I was at a spiritual festival doing appearances, signing books and so on, and having a chat with my publisher when we fell into discussion about these communities — he had experienced them, too. I mentioned that I would love to create something that held the soul frequency of this tribal wisdom, that could support those communities and could be shared with others. He loved the idea, so I opened my heart and mind to it. Not long after that, I discovered the work of Isabel Bryna. In her images, I instantly felt the frequency of the soul tribe consciousness that I loved and valued so much. I messaged her about becoming involved, and she agreed. And so, the oracle deck and journal dedicated to earth warriors were born.

In the pages of this journal, you will find four healing processes. These can be done at any time you are drawn to do so. They can be done relatively quickly, or you can go deep and take longer if you choose. Set aside some time for yourself, turn off your mobile phone and other devices, keep the lighting soft and wear comfortable clothing. Aiming for a space where you can go into your journey and not be distracted by the external world. If you are unable to create an ideal space, the healing processes will do their work. You can come back to the processes as often as you wish.

I hope you find comfort, encouragement, sacred feminine wisdom and soul nourishment through your work with this journal. You have an earth warrior within, one who understands that you must create your own life, and respect and guide your own communities from a place of heart wisdom. May this journal be a place to reinforce the value and worth of your intuition and the guiding inner wisdom of the Universe that every day reminds us we have the power to protect, heal, create and regenerate our own bodies, minds and lives, as well as our world and all the beings in it, for the greatest good, from a place of love.

Namaste,

Alana

The power and ways are given to us to be passed on to others.
— Fools Crow, Ceremonial Chief, Teton Sioux

There is a river flowing now very fast. It is so great and swift that there are those who will be afraid. They will try to hold on to the shore. They will feel they are torn apart and will suffer greatly.

Know the river has its destination. The elders say we must let go of the shore, push off into the middle of the river, keep our eyes open, and our heads above water. And I say, see who is in there with you and celebrate. At this time in history, we are to take nothing personally, least of all ourselves. For the moment that we do, our spiritual growth and journey comes to a halt.

The time for the lone wolf is over. Gather yourselves! Banish the word 'struggle' from your attitude and your vocabulary. All that we do now must be done in a sacred manner and in celebration.

We are the ones we've been waiting for.

— attributed to an unnamed Hopi elder, Hopi Nation, Oraibi, Arizona

The battle cry of Earth's wise children unites us all. It evokes a passionate response from Spirit that brings sacred healing grace to our cause.

The Beauty Way reminds you that beneath the noise, beneath your worries and concerns, there is oneness between you and life. Even if your world feels chaotic at times, even if you fear you have gone off track, the path that will return you to peace, beauty, balance and harmony is always here for you.

Problems will often disappear altogether when you relax your mind and heart. In opening to Great Spirit, you shall realise many problems were nothing more than the dark creation of an overworked, fatigued mind, negatively fantasising about something that need never happen.

When some form of ugliness is disturbing your soul, threatening to steal your peaceful trust in the Divine, you are guided to come back to the Beauty Way, back into worshipful reverence of the sacred. From that place, you are empowered to deal with the situation in a way that increases love and joy in yourself and the world.

Can you relax for a moment now? This is your first step into the Beauty Way. Allow the simple beauty of nature, of human kindness, of divine love to seep deep into your soul … infusing it like a sacred tea.

If we are struggling with change — either too much or too little of it — let us be reassured. When something is in need of repair, Great Spirit knows how to restore it. When something needs to end, Great Spirit will show the way to empty ourselves of the past and prepare for a new beginning.

We do not need to fear change, whether wanted or unwanted. We just
need to trust in the good and loving workings of the Universe.

Evolution is not always easy — it often requires tremendous courage of
heart and inner strength. Yet, we belong to life and can trust in it.

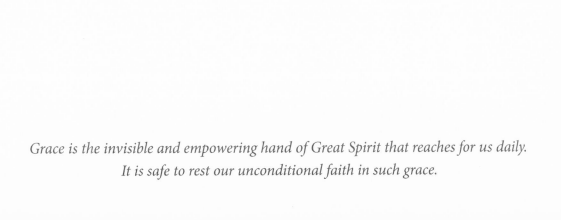

Grace is the invisible and empowering hand of Great Spirit that reaches for us daily.
It is safe to rest our unconditional faith in such grace.

A prayer for renewal: "All that I need to support my evolution into the next expression of my divine destiny is generously provided for me. I now surrender into this divine blessing for renewal, open to receive for my highest good. So be it."

I am Puma. I awaken within you the vigorous energy, fierce power and ability to act without hesitation when the moment is right. My patience and strategy, my preparation and precision, my fearlessness and decisiveness are now your own.
— A medicine blessing from Puma

Apply yourself fully to the task. Let go of old ways of viewing yourself as incapable, scattered or wasteful of energy. You can focus intently, generate clear intention and achieve your ambitions through methodical steps and applied will.

Healing Process
THE BEAUTY WAY

For those times when the ugliness of ego threatens to steal your joy and trust.

⟵—◈✦◈—⟶

Take a moment to write down what you would like to transform from ugliness into beauty through divine wisdom. It may be an issue you are struggling to accept or a problem you feel needs more light and healing.

Say: "*Today I open myself to the generosity and grace of the Universe in all ways, and specifically offer this sacred ritual to the Divine Mother, so that there may be healing for* (read your list of issues). *May I always be part of a loving, inspired solution. So be it.*"

Stand comfortably in the 'centre' of your healing space. Place your hand on your heart and read the following prayer aloud, as you follow the accompanying directions.

> *Today I walk the Beauty Way,*
> *All darkness and evil depart.*
> *I now become beauty and peace,*
> *With the cool breeze of divine grace renewing me from within.*
> *My thoughts and my words are beautiful.*
> *Nothing shall hinder my reverence and ease.*
> *All day I walk the Beauty Way.*

Turn to the east (or your right). Say aloud: "*The children of the earth are beautiful and blessed with wisdom. Care is given to all beings of the earth that are vulnerable and in need of divine protection. They play in divine beauty.*"

Turn to the south (or turn again to your right). Say aloud: "*The young people of the earth are beautiful and blessed with wisdom. The flow of life energy is aligned with divine will to benefit all, for the greatest good. They dance in divine beauty."*

Turn to the west (or turn again to your right). Say aloud: *"The parents of the earth are beautiful and blessed with wisdom. Spiritual strength and true guardianship of all earth's beings prevail. They love in divine beauty."*

Turn to the North (or turn again to your right). Say aloud: *"The grandparents of the earth are beautiful and blessed with wisdom. Guidance is given and heeded to create harmony, peace and beauty between all peoples and the earth. They rest in divine beauty."*

Standing in the centre, say the following aloud: *"I walk with beauty before me. I walk with beauty behind me. I walk with beauty below me. I walk with beauty above me. I walk with beauty all around me and within every part of my soul."*

Take a moment to feel connected to your heart. Believe in the power of your words. Feel what it is like to trust in the healing divine beauty that flows in you and throughout all of life.

Take the piece of paper with the issues on it and crumble it up in your hands. Say aloud:

"The Universe is generous and wise. Healing for these matters in my own mind and in the world, is now flowing. So be it."

You may like to rip the piece of paper into bits, to burn it or to place it in the recycling bin (which is symbolic spiritually as well as practical and helpful for the environment!). Notice your mindset shift into more compassion, and new ways of thinking and responding over the coming days and weeks ahead. You have completed your healing process.

*Give yourself the chance to use your power in a safe and wise way.
This right use of power — surrendered and in service to the great
power of the Divine — will help you overcome your reluctance and lay
claim to your will. You need your will to transform inspiration into
action. The world truly needs this from you.*

Whatever it is you dream of attaining or desire to do in this world, Puma medicine fills your soul with this message, "You have the power."

*The ancient guardian mother protects the waters of life and offers her
protection and blessing. Her appearance augurs a time of purification
and cleansing that leads to enhanced fertility. Her oracle for you now
is to trust in the resourcefulness of your creativity.*

Whilst it is important to engage with others, the sacred creator within you requires time and space in solitude to process, reflect, contemplate and create. Only then can you remember who you are, know what is important to you and summon the inner power to act accordingly.

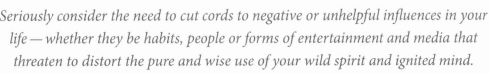

Seriously consider the need to cut cords to negative or unhelpful influences in your life — whether they be habits, people or forms of entertainment and media that threaten to distort the pure and wise use of your wild spirit and ignited mind.

*Give yourself a chance for spiritual, psychological and emotional
time out and cleansing so that you can recognise the inner truth
of your soul and adhere to it faithfully.*

What original healing stories will you give birth to in your life and in this world?

If you have lost the zest for your passion, or have become confused, overwhelmed or scattered with too many ideas or directions, give yourself space and time for renewal. Allow any 'overload' of mind or nervous system to discharge intearth.

The waters of your consciousness must be safeguarded,
so they can become a tonic for the souls of others.

Vigorously contest any who attempt to exploit, direct or distort
the true expression of your higher knowing.

As you allow purity to emerge from deeply restful and reflective meditation, your personal energy and spiritual potency grow. Your potential to be an influence in this world increases accordingly.

Avoid being manipulated by negative energies by refusing to entertain any person or idea that drains, depletes or diminishes the quality of your consciousness. Be resolute and exacting. If it's not right, courageously and unapologetically cast it out.

Instead of contorting yourself to fit into the frustrated and grasping world of others, offer those seeking something more beautiful the opportunity to find refuge within your world. Instead of being influenced, become an influencer. Instead of trying to dominate others, awaken in them the desire for their own higher nature.

It takes courage to refuse to bow down to productivity pushers who aren't interested in authentic offerings that heal through the process of their creation as well as in their final form. They just want more stuff to perpetuate conveyer-belt consumerism for the genuine benefit of no one. Your refusals are sacred.

A prayer for wise global resource management: "Divine Mother, please help humankind to understand and implement the best ways to protect the natural resources of this planet. May we use the creative power of our consciousness with wild and loving reverence for life, to generate wise action and purify the waters of spiritual grace to restore all beings thirsty for truth."

Fear not. Pray boldly and be faithful. All is well.

Healing Process
THE CIRCLE CROSS OF TENAN

For when you need a sacred convergence, a rare intersection of heaven and earth.

⟵ ◈ ◈ ⟶

There are times when heaven and earth align, and the power unleashed is considerable. As if by a miracle, patience, persistence, effort and energy finally come together — people rally, situations fall into place and creations of tangible goodness take shape in the world. It can be unexpected. You may have almost given up hope, then suddenly, everything comes together. The Circle Cross of Tenan signals such a happening in your world … a moment of powerful grace, where Spirit makes its presence felt upon the earth.

The priestess who bridges heaven and earth, dwells within Tenan, the lunar pyramid of the ancient city of Teotihuacán, with the circle cross as her guide. She intuitively knows when and how to call for heavenly assistance, as all priestesses do. Part of her role is to pray for those in her spiritual care, invoking divine love and requesting heavenly assistance and grace for all living beings. It is her spiritual responsibility to keep the channels between heaven and earth not only open, but healthy and robust, active and stable. Why? Because she is capable of doing so. This is your sacred role, also.

This exercise will guide you to tap in to divine frequencies, to pray to the unconditionally loving divine source for all events and for all beings — perhaps through a specific event or situation that you know needs healing change.

You can create your own circle cross or gaze at the image below. If you wish to create your own, you can do this with small crystals, rope, scarves, candles or by drawing it on paper. You may want to dance or sing your circle cross into being, too. Your circle cross is a portal or altar through which you can focus on, and be receptive to, the intersection of Great Spirit and Mother Earth for divine alignment, healing and recalibration.

When you feel that your circle cross is open, it is time to activate it. Stand near or in it, as feels right for you.

Turn to the east (or your right) and say: *"Through the protective gateway of unconditional love, I invite the power of divine grace into my being and into this world."*

Turn to the south (or turn again to your right) and say aloud: *"Through the protective gateway of unconditional love, I invite the power of divine will into my being and into this world."*

Turn to the west (or turn again to your right) and say: *"Through the protective gateway of unconditional love, I invite the power of divine healing into my being and into this world."*

Turn to the north (or turn again to your right) and say aloud: *"Through the protective gateway of unconditional love, I invite the power of divine presence into my being and into this world."*

Direct your attention to the ground beneath your feet and say aloud: *"Earth Mother, may all of humanity love, honour and protect you. Thank you for all that you do for us. You are a Buddha Mother of creativity, generosity and wild grace."*

If there is a specific situation or circumstance you wish to open to divine realignment, say the following prayer: *"I offer this situation to the Divine for realignment, through the ageless wisdom and celestial power of divine love* (describe the situation you wish to offer up for healing). *I now release this for the greatest good."* Imagine or intend that you are releasing it to the Universe for healing now.

Put your attention on the sky above your head and say aloud: *"On behalf of all humanity, I invoke divine love, light and wisdom for the fulfilment of purpose for all divine beings. May we be assisted through the endless divine resource for the greatest good for all generations. May divine grace evoke love and higher consciousness in all realms. It is done."*

Finish by placing your hands in prayer and bowing your head.

You are part of a team of souls working to keep the balance of light on our planet intact, accessible and vital. Offer yourself to the divine plan without holding anything back and know that you shall be helped in countless ways, just as you offer your own will and talent to the sacred purpose of healing in this world.

If you have experienced great struggle or loss, the spirit medicine of Butterfly brings hopeful promise to your heart. Here is your sign that there will be happiness, peace and light. Trust in the goodness being birthed.

You are not meant to turn to the past, as it cannot support you the way it once did. Trust in what is happening, even whilst you don't fully understand it. It will turn out beautifully in the end — which will also be a new beginning.

There are moments when even those of us with great courage feel tested beyond our faith. Doubt, darkness and despair can creep into our minds and lash our hearts with fear. Yet the soul needs faith and hope like the body needs air to breathe. Let your soul believe in the goodness and grace of Great Spirit ... always at work, in all things, in all ways.

You do not have to regret anything that has happened. You do not have to judge yourself or any other, nor wish that things had been different. You have not missed out. You have not messed up. You have been learning and growing.

Like a butterfly that crawls on the ground like a caterpillar, there will come a time when you will have outgrown your old ways of being. It will be time, instead, to trust your wings and learn how to be in a new way.

In the divine alchemy of transformation things sometimes appear to be going backwards as they move forward. After summer there is autumn and then winter, all of which indicate progress towards the next spring. Your soul is a natural creature and the sacred laws of nature govern its process, too.

If you didn't understand the creative purpose and regenerative nature of the seasons, you might be frightened by the winter, concerned that it signified the world was ending! With knowledge of the seasons, you are not afraid of winter — you see it as an essential part of life. You may even learn to nurture and restore yourself during that time, gaining conscious benefit and appreciation for it.

Let your heart and mind rest in the trust that life is growing your
soul into beautiful fulfilment.

Transformation into full maturity involves learning how to grow through light and through darkness back to the light again. You will always find your way back to the light. Have faith in yourself and what must be. Dedicate yourself to what you love without hesitation.

Sometimes things seem to be working against us. It is only later that they show themselves to have been valuable ways of acquiring the greater faith, courage and determination necessary for the fulfilment of our purpose.

Keep going. Everything happening in your life is helping you fulfil your divine potential. Know that any darkness will give way to the light.

Having faith in your own purpose when it feels like you are fighting a losing battle takes a lot of heart. Great Spirit knows what you are up to and wants to remind you that you are not being foolish — you are following your destiny.

You are meant to be a light in this world, and it is important that you allow Great Spirit to support you in this task. Safeguarding your state of mind is essential for you to accomplish your life purpose. If you get caught up in negative thinking — as may happen from time to time — allow Great Spirit to guide you back to the truth of your inner light.

We are meant to call upon the Universe for assistance in all ways possible. We are meant to use our strengths of love, compassion, wisdom, light and kindness to be kickass earth warriors who will never give up, and who are smart enough to use every resource we can to affirm priorities that honour life. In this way, we uplift ourselves and inspire others through our life journey.

There are dark forces that want you to lose hope, because they know you are unstoppable when your heart is hopeful. Leave the Divine to deal with such darkness and tend to the light of hope in your heart.

Healing Process

WHAT MUST BE, SHALL BE

For keeping the faith when things seem to be working against you.

—◈—

Just as life and death are natural, so too is growth. It is natural for the caterpillar to become the butterfly. If we really think about it, it is extraordinary to the point of being almost unbelievable, but it is natural nonetheless. So, it is meant to be that with human life there is loss that becomes part of the process allowing for something new to be vitalised. This is how the soul grows. Just like the seemingly impossible journey of the butterfly. With sacred endings that support new beginnings, you too are moving through the cycle of life.

Sometimes this can be confronting. To give up old ways or old identities can seem frightening to the mind. It may seem as though you are being asked to give up too much to secure your goals. You may wonder if it is foolish imagination rather than genuine soul purpose that is driving you forward.

Great Spirit wants you to accept that it can help you, that what you are pursuing is meant to be and that success will come when you keep to your course. Allow the inner force that compels you forward to have its way. Do not fear the sometimes-radical changes that take place as you evolve into your destiny. Any losses or endings along the way are essential for your fulfilment.

Say this prayer aloud: *"I call upon the wild grace of the sacred feminine and give gratitude for your wise and loving assistance in my life. I accept your blessing to fulfil my soul purpose for the highest good, and to help all beings fulfil the plan Great Spirit has placed in our hearts. Only the goodness of your wisdom and protection prevails, and every darkness leads me into greater light."*

Take some time to reflect on what it is you feel or sense is happening within your soul at this time. Are you opening up, trusting more, and loving more? Are you letting an old version of yourself fall away, even though this may scare you? Perhaps you are learning to trust that what is in your heart does matter and that the Universe supports the fulfilment of your divine potential. Speak about it or write about it now. Give yourself a chance to let go of burdens, to express and release your soul through an authentic conversation with the Universe.

Finish with this short prayer to your own soul: *"My dear soul, you know what you are doing and how to grow in harmony with divine genius and sacred purpose, even when my conscious mind does not understand. You know, when I do not know. So, I choose to trust you. The Universe is on our side, and this brings me peace and comfort now. I trust you."*

Place your hands in prayer at your heart and bow your head. Allow yourself to sense, feel or imagine how much love, care and help Great Spirit has already set in motion for you. When you are ready, just finish your healing process by saying thank you to your soul and the Universe.

A prayer for when you've picked up something energetically that really doesn't belong to you. Repeat three times, "Through unconditional divine love and my own free will, I surrender that which is not rightfully mine."

A sacred ritual to call in your blessings. Place your hands in front of your heart, with the palms facing up as if to receive. Say aloud, with gratitude, "The divine blesses me. I am filled and blessed."

The Universe does not want to be limited to repeating what has already been. Newness needs to burst through you into startling expressions of abundant life. You are guided into unknown territory, directed beyond all you have known yourself and your world to be, so that something original and necessary can be brought to life.

If you have been in lack, limitation or anxiety, relax and substitute your stress for the absolute trust that the Universe will provide all good things with generosity and grace. If you find this challenging, take it one step at a time by reprogramming your heart and mind into new habits of peaceful trust. Living like this will feel much better and bring better results, too.

Know that the provision of all necessary resources is a certainty. The only variables are the details of how the journey unfolds. Trust the Universe.

Kumu *is the Hawaiian term for teacher and source of wisdom. The Universe is the great kumu. When we trust in the Universe, we come to understand certain truths and realise we don't have to be limited to what we logically know. If we are willing to expand our faith, then that which we can experience in harmony with the Universe will expand, also.*

Your beautiful and perhaps impossible-seeming dreams are supported by the unlimited resources of the Universe. Even if you don't know what is needed to create a successful outcome, the Universe does.

Don't allow your mind to create visions of poverty, lack, failure or absence of support. Focus instead upon the sweet generosity of the Universe and all that is lovingly providing for you. Often, without you consciously realising what you need, all that is necessary for your best life and fulfilment of your sacred purpose is gifted in advance.

You can lend your energy, your mind and your body to what you want to have happen in this world. The Universe will hear and feel you and provide resources accordingly. Let your thoughts and hopes become your prayers, and the answers to those prayers will benefit all life on this planet.

An abundance prayer to remind you to relax and enjoy the journey:
"I am so grateful for the generosity, abundance and attentiveness of
the Universe. My needs are provided for with such grace and love. All
resources for my life purpose to be successfully and joyfully expressed
are freely given to me. May all beings consciously know the loving
embrace of the Universe and fulfil their sacred purpose. So be it."

A sacred ritual for abundance. Relax for a moment with your hands in prayer at your heart. Imagine that the generous, wise, loving and joyful universal energy is overflowing within your heart.

You are sensitive, and rightly so. Never judge your sensitivity or feel that you are overreacting, but also allow nature to calm and soothe you so you can focus on accomplishing your soul mission.

Allow the Divine Mother to be your friend and guide whilst trusting that more allies will arrive at the right moment. The Earth Mother has her own sense of timing, and you are not forgotten. You are just growing according to her wisdom and grace. Have faith in yourself and in her.

Healing Process

IXCHEL AND THE MEDICINE OF THE RAINBOW JAGUAR

For when you need to summon divine badassery and cut something from your life.

—◈✦◈—

Using her rainbow jaguar medicine, the Mayan minx of midwifery and medicine, Ixchel, instructs your soul to fearlessly confront that which is unworthy of your devotion, thus eradicating destructive forces and creating space for healing relief and rebirth. Her presence is the wild power of the jaguar within, the rainbow's promise of renewal and the divine feminine protection of the sacred midwife who is the guardian of transitions into new life. She brings the message that there are times when fierceness is necessary.

It is important that you cut off negative sources completely at this time and do not allow yourself to be used or exploited. This is not the time to indulge someone else's ego or go against your inner knowing to give someone the benefit of the doubt. Trust your instincts and break immediately from what isn't right for you. Have the courage of your convictions.

Jaguar is not a half-way medicine. If we allow unworthy influences to take up residence in our minds, our hearts, our souls — even just a little — they will eventually be our undoing, eroding our happiness, self-esteem, vitality and ability to fulfil our passionate purpose. Ixchel brings Jaguar to remind us that exploitation, abuse and disrespect are unacceptable and must be dealt with effectively, according to correct timing and with absolute certainty in our hearts. This is not about harming another but about cutting off their influence in our souls.

Find a place to relax. Feel or imagine a rainbow starting at your left side, arcing over your head and landing on your right side. The right side then arcs underneath you and joins back up with the start of the rainbow on your left. You now have an oval rainbow shape around you.

Say aloud: *"The rainbow light now brings me healing, blessing and spiritual grace, in accord with unconditional divine love. The Divine Mother brings me all I need with such generosity and wisdom."*

Rest in this rainbow light, allowing it to bring you healing. Simply relax for as long as feels right. When you are ready, say aloud, *"Jaguar medicine honours my soul and divine love, now."*

What needs to be cut from your life? Reflect on what needs to be severed through jaguar medicine. Remember, this is never about someone else not being good enough. You can love and have compassion for someone or something and still recognise that certain behaviours or influences are not right for you, in your life, at this time. Often, it is an attitude or behaviour within our own minds that is the real culprit in our unhappiness. It may lead us to believe that we deserve to be punished, are not worthy of respect, or that we should sacrifice our needs for love, affection and protection so that someone else can continue behaving dishonourably. You may have the spiritual maturity to recognise that when you change the way you feel about yourself and sever negative or victimising choices from your soul, that any negative forces in your life will lose their capacity to influence you.

When you are ready say: *"I invite Rainbow Jaguar Healing Medicine to protect my soul from harm, for the greatest good, so be it."*

Imagine, feel or pretend that you allow what you have reflected upon to be consumed in the rainbow fire of Ixchel's Medicine Jaguar. It doesn't need to take long. Jaguar is swift and precise.

Bring your attention back to the rainbow light that surrounds you. Allow it to concentrate itself gently into the depths of your soul, helping you to integrate the changes and balance your body, mind and soul. Rest for as long as you need. You have completed your healing process.

What means so much to you that you are willing to give up all you have held on to out of fear so that it may be? What matters enough that you will endure transformation — with all the endings and uncertainty such growth entails — so that your dream can become real? Let the power of your passion give you courage and the Universe will rally to your cause!

From a place of wisdom rather than fearfulness, take heed of the energy you allow to have direct and unfettered access to your inner being. A position of such influence over your state of mind is best reserved for the Divine.

You will know when a message is authentically divine. You will feel happy, at peace, willing and capable, even in the face of challenge. Genuine divine guidance does not create anxiety, nor does it paint something to be well when it needs repair. Yet, no matter the content of the message, you will feel relief in the face of such loving and helpful truth.

A sacred ritual for when it all seems a bit too much. Assume a relaxed, comfortable position. Sit or lie down wrapped up in a blanket or shawl; or hug yourself, nestle next to your pet, or stretch out delightedly on your back like a star fish. Rest for as long as feels right for you.

Seek what feels true, even beyond the logical. If something doesn't feel right, challenge it and dig deeper. Enhance your self-esteem by researching information and trusting your intuition to help you discern what is useful and true. Trust the power of your mind to receive and recognise the answers you need. You will find your way.

Intuition and instinct are forms of sacred feminine knowing. One arises from the heart and the other from the wisdom of the body. You do not need to have a logical explanation to justify your intuitive and instinctive recognition of falsehood, deception or other misleading uses of information. These special forms of knowing are essential to a wise and authentic life.

Sometimes intuition and instinct will tell you a piece of information
accepted by others is not actually true for you.

The judgements of others — for better or worse — are meaningless.
What matters is that you find your own best way of sensing truth,
honouring when something does not feel right and moving forward
when something rings true.

Reach out for help from others, whilst you honour and respect your individuality and your unique life journey. Balance social time with taking care of your own individual needs, including the need for time out in solitude to hear your inner truths and to renew yourself.

Anger can be a sign from the soul — a sacred gift that asks you to deal with
a situation to bring about something different and more empowering.
Use your anger as a sacred gift with compassion and clear purpose.

Fight wholeheartedly when you need to safeguard what truly matters.

Be open to a greater guiding wisdom so you know when to be merciful
and when to cut something off completely.

Believe in the power of your inner voice and do not silence yourself.

The howling wolf brings medicine for standing your ground and defending that which is rightfully within your guardianship. Using your voice and your energy to set boundaries and claim your space is important. The territory is not physical. That is the way of the ego. The territory is spiritual. Claiming it means reclaiming and sustaining the right state of mind and openheartedness, protecting your soul space for all beings that seek refuge within it.

You belong to the Clan of the Wolf Heart. Wolf medicine is the awakening of the pathfinder, the way-shower and the teacher. Wolf can learn new ways and teach them to others. Part of your soul purpose is to guide and inspire others through what you learn to master in your life.

Believe in the power of the Divine to keep an eye on things for you. Trust that power to alert you when you need to know something or to understand what is happening in your life and what you need to do or not do. Practice feeling confidence and unconditional trust in a higher power. Know it is stronger than all else.

*Don't avoid the spotlight, nor try to hide yourself, nor dull your light
to appease another or your own fears. Your true inner beauty and
divine light is meant to help others, and the only way that can occur is
if you allow yourself to be seen.*

Trying to blend in will drain the energy from you. Let those who are attracted to your light adapt to your level of divine expression. You are the benchmark, and they will evolve to reach you.

Condor swiftly brings the will of Great Spirit to Earth, through the gift of powerful medicine. Despite great odds, even in the face of what may appear to be an inevitable defeat, extraordinary triumph is at hand. This is the prophecy of resurrection, of the rising up of what was thought to be lost.

The Divine Feminine Oracle gives prophesy for your healing. Abuela Medicina, the remedy of the Grandmother Spirits, is with you. What is needed to heal your body, mind and soul shall come to you. Pray with faith for what you need to be granted and keep your heart and mind open to the loving guidance that will teach you all you need to know.